I'd Rather Be a Hyacinth

poems by

Cathy Hailey

Finishing Line Press
Georgetown, Kentucky

"*The poet, being an imitator like a painter or any other artist, must of necessity imitate one of three objects—things as they were or are, things as they are said or thought to be, or things as they ought to be.*"

—Aristotle, *Poetics*

I'd Rather Be a Hyacinth

For my daughter,
Alexandra "Zan" Delaine Hailey,
poet, visual artist, dancer,
1992-2018

ACKNOWLEDGMENTS

Thank you to the editors of the following publications, in which these poems
appeared:

"500,000" was published in *The New Verse News*, edited by James Penha,
February 25, 2021.

An earlier version of "Circling Back" was published under the title "Tracing
His Past" in *NoVA Bards 2021*, edited by Nick Hale, published by Local
Gems Press, September 16, 2021.

"Under the Sun" was published along with Roberta Thole's painting, Golden
Urns, in *Springtime in Winter: An Ekphrastic Study in Art, Poetry, and Music*,
edited by Mike Maggio and designed by Antonella Manganelli.

Publisher: Leah Huete de Maines
Editor: Christen Kincaid
Cover Art: Cathy Hailey
Author Photo: Katie Peterson
Cover Design: Elizabeth Maines McCleavy

Order online: www.finishinglinepress.com
            also available on amazon.com

Author inquiries and mail orders:
Finishing Line Press
PO Box 1626
Georgetown, Kentucky 40324
USA

Table of Contents

Morendo

Under the Sun
after Roberta Thole's Golden Urns

Helios ascends,
bursting urns of golden fire,
glazing graceful winds.

Rhapsodizing lyre
song, strummed by Apollo's hand,
transcends bound canvas.

Mirrored vases stand—
secular iconostas—
framing Truth's tableau.

Are laurel leaves live
when captured on urn's glow?
Do chariot's rise?

Mimesis awaits motion—
artistic contradiction.

Sun-Drenched

Spring sunbath—eyes close,
head tilting toward noonday sun.
Eye kaleidoscope

creates cordovan,
crimson, rust, rose ebony—
color change in reds,

rare serenity.
Slight eye movements beneath lids
give birth to yellow

lake, forest mirrored.
Shapes reverberate, echo,
replicate; glittered

lenses convex to concave—
sunshine's psychedelic rave.

Falling Rose
> *after* The Rose Adagio *from Act I of* The Sleeping Beauty

Crowned with twisted braids,
sequined glimmer tulle tutus,
spinning silver threads,

weave between tall boots.
Muscles pulse with each sauté,
grande jeté, sissonne.

Vests of gold lamé
feathered cavalier hats donned,
partnering begins.

Passing pink tutus,
taking turns with timely spins—
fouettés like corkscrews.

Though each suitor gifts a rose,
Beauty falls into repose.

Dad, Brother, and Me
South Glebe Road, 1960s

Ping-pong, tetherball,
and basketball O'Leary
till the dinner call.

Fitness by burpee.
Go out for a pass, Dad shouts,
football spiraling.

Scouring for bike parts—
fix-it lessons for cycling—
junkyard treasure smiles.

Mowing summer grass,
raking leaves in giant piles—
long as we could last.

We vie to be dominant.
He teaches: be confident.

Blue Prince

after The Quatre

Whimsical music
ushers the blue prince on stage—
movement majestic.

Radchenko's mélange—
leading jewel-skirted ladies—
pas de deux times two.

Magical decrees,
poses to whisper adieu
challenge gravity.

Mirror imagery,
carnival festivity,
pink camaraderie—

dancers pirouette around,
lift and lower to the ground.

Seduction

Bluebirds ring pie tin
lured by raspberry fruit bars,
walnuts, plumped raisins.

Like textile bazaars—
sequined, indigo feathered,
glint sun flare, snow glare,

flying untethered,
blue variations so rare.
Breasts beige and ochre

contrast, enhancing
turquoise tail feather flicker.
Shyly accepting

entrapment and seduction
for my artistic passion.

Poseidon's Province

after The Ocean and the Pearls *from* The Little Humpbacked Horse

Red dress, light tan vest,
alternate in pointe solo—
energy then rest—

ending in tableau.
Mermaids deep in salty sea
beckoning backward

in spun fleur de lis.
Grand jeté, oceans conquered.
Turns in unison,

red cummerbunds mime,
longing to reach each maiden
as triangles chime.

Red organza peasant dress,
lifted up as muscles press.

Circling Back
Ocean City, MD

Distorted magic,
fun house carnival mirrors,
Wurlitzer music

draw him to Trimper's
historical carousel,
summer fairy tales,

where carved creatures dwell—
turquoise sea serpents, curled tails,
bearing tongue and teeth,

stately ribboned steeds,
cascading rose wreaths,
in fixed canter leads—

creatures his sister cherished,
ride shared before she perished.

Enchantment
> *after* Adagio *from Act III of* Cinderella

Awakening from
princely dreams in black and white—
a far-off kingdom

in the dark of night—
no monochromatic world—
colorful dancing

goddesses unfurled
still hopeful for romancing
till Cinderella

captivates the prince
of honor at the gala,
then flees in silence.

After a successful chase,
the pas de deux, interlaced.

White-Breasted Nuthatches

Wall walking edges,
corners of portico bricks,
lookout on ledges,

performing wry tricks,
our upside-down acrobats
shinnying down trunks.

Forest habitats
furnish foraging for chunks
of tree nuts, acorns,

wedged in, hacked open.
Nasal calls—staccato horns—
enchant mates chosen,

fated cavity nesters,
woodpecker hole subletters.

Chiaroscuro
after Adagio *from* Romeo and Juliet

Beauty juxtaposed
against darkest irony;
tragedy unfolds.

From her balcony
she dreamed of his sweet embrace:
dancers mirroring

leaps and turns with grace
despite families feuding
with harsh resentment.

In tunic and tights,
romantic movement
through darkest nights,

sharing dominance in love
as spirits ascend above.

500,000

Ascent and descent—
symmetrical staircases
move candlelight bent.

Flames flicker faces,
pathways towards transcendency,
spirits drifting in

liminality.
A presidential burden
despite empathy

comforts multitudes
in national eulogy,
church bell interludes,

ritual "Amazing Grace."
All, *Recquiesat en Pace.*

Animando

Fancy
after Grand Pas *from Act III of* Don Quixote

Matador jacket,
red skinny tie, red flowers,
sleeves of black fishnet.

Amplitude, power,
posing high and posing low,
reaching for windmills.

Spinning fast and slow,
ascending life's highest hills,
man of La Mancha.

Synchronizing feet
with athletic stamina,
punctuating beat.

Lyrical percussionist—
red fan, a flick of his wrist.

Flight

Butterfly remnants
grounded in cotton batting,
labeled specimens—

midlife traveling
father reaching out for love
with exotic wings.

Daughter now above
without her silver earrings—
worn by her father—

a gift less fragile,
his gesture meant to honor,
revive her dazzle,

will her fire to ignite.
Butterflies are meant for flight.

Coquettes

after Pas de Quatre

Just off the shoulders,
ruffled sleeves, deep sweetheart necks,
posed in white layers,

four dancers connect
in floral celebration—
sensuality,

frenzied flirtation
graces natural gaiety
of white butterflies—

artists on trapeze.
Nature's true passions arise
on billowing breeze.

Heliotropic flowers
pose as sensual powers.

Romance Remembered

Tea kettle whistles,
inviting afternoon tea.
Mom reminisces:

youth in New Jersey,
single life in Manhattan,
Greek circle dancing,

wedding in satin,
jitterbug swing enhancing
island honeymoon.

Romance for hours,
Alexa playing her tunes
crooning their amours.

She reminds me to write all
before she cannot recall.

Ethereal
after Allegro

A solo— a tease—
unison from toes to heels,
tighten then release

in circular reels.
Surrounded by her footmen,
lifting to heaven,

angel of passion
blinking stars interwoven.
Celestial doll,

stiffening her stance,
purple perky parasol,
tutu of romance.

Powering with deep knee bend,
men propel her dive to end.

Flying High

Yellow pigments fade
as our rose opens wider,
till petals cascade.

Rainstorm denied her
a lifeline earned and deserved.
Gerbera daisies,

magenta, preserved,
stand tall like charming ladies
in crowds of proud leaves.

How does God decide
which flower stays, which recedes?
Mother Nature's chide?

Darwin's law does not apply.
She lived as a butterfly.

Metamorphosis
after Dying Swan

Radiant whiteness,
lights fusing iridescence
on lustrous tresses.

The lake's ambience
inspires the sleek white bird.
Hyperflexible

human arms convert
to wings—supple, pliable—
bending then folding.

Preening swan plumage,
Odette dreams up dazzling
future self-image—

a stately mademoiselle—
freedom from his savage spell.

Hurricane Camille

South Glebe Road, August 1969

Hop the fence; don't fall.
Head across the field to our creek
where cattails grow tall,

beckon hide and seek,
where water specimens grow
amoeba and stink.

Waters trickling low,
surging high over the brink
turning field to lake,

basements to deep pools,
drowning beloved keepsakes,
darkening our moods.

Interruption of childhood,
erasure of neighborhood.

Enigma

after Selections from Paquita

A man's world of war—
Napoleonic Army—
crossed with gypsy lore.

With no pedigree
this undignified woman
is no soldier's wife.

Grace of a heron,
saves the soldier losing life
by switching glasses,

avoiding poison,
cruel economic clashes.
Her gold medallion,

proof of noble position,
inspires love proposition.

Merrymaking

A splatting sunbath,
squirrel stretched over
tabletop wood slats,

still life performer—
rainstorm's aftermath—
warming up to me.

Eying their flightpath
from apple tree canopy,
I catch glinting gold

finches feeding low,
thistle fiesta unfolds—
Cinco de Mayo.

Cheery garden performers—
my happiness restorers.

In Life…

Hyacinths, purple—
baby blooms adding stress, weight—
instinct maternal.

Tulips variegate
orange-yellow, dancing, coy,
above troupes of green,

singular pride, joy
even with no breeze
In life, I'd rather

be a hyacinth,
embrace the role of mother,
live the labyrinth,

loved by a brood of florets—
barycenter of orbits.

Afterword

In Closing

To curb long-winded
verse—haiku, haiku sonnet—
excess rescinded.

Villanelle, sonnet—
iambic pentameter
counting tens and fives

or a repeater
color coding special lines
tercets to quatrain.

Limits help us grow,
when we push beyond brain strain,
writing poems that glow.

There's magic in condensing,
precision in expressing.

The Haiku Sonnet

I discovered the haiku sonnet form in Tom Hunley's *The Poetry Gymnasium*. Hunley invented this hybrid form, a marriage of eastern and western poetic styles, which incorporates four haiku and a couplet (or three haiku and a tanka) and the rhyme scheme of the Shakespearean sonnet. I've enjoyed the challenge of writing haiku sonnets, and the practice has served me well in honing my language and reining in sprawling prose.

Notes

Ten haiku sonnets are ekphrastic poems inspired by a performance of Moscow Festival Ballet's *Ballet Favorites and Great Moments* I attended on April 6, 2014, at George Mason University's Center for the Arts. Ballet scene titles from the program appear under the poem titles.

Roberta Thole's painting, "Golden Urns," can be viewed on p. 39 of *Viva Reston Lifestyle Magazine*, January-February 2017, at https://issuu.com/vivatysons/docs/2017-01_janfeb. The image accompanies Alessandra Rossi's article, "Poets and Painters Collaboration at the Reston Art Gallery."

Gratitude

I'd like to thank those who supported me in the stepping stones through my writing journey:

My parents: Dad who loved words and taught me revision in elementary school; Mom who started my education in the library and allowed me to be messy in the kitchen and my "art studio."

My husband, Ken, who inspired me as an artist and guided my process.

Our children, Alexandra and Neil, who spent four years in my creative writing classes and taught me as much as I taught them. Both became poets, writers, creators, careful readers of my work, and encouraged my creative passions. Alexandra became Poet Laureate of Prince William County, 2014-16. Neil is an entrepreneur, a 3D printing enthusiast, who thrives in creativity.

My brother, Michael, his family, and the extended family I've spent holidays with for constant support.

My sister-in-law, Katie, for her exceptional photography.

Teachers from first grade through graduate school who allowed me to write, challenged me to improve, and inspired my love of writing.

Colleagues of the Northern Virginia Writing Project (NVWP) at George Mason University, especially those who taught in the Student Summer Institute and Young Writers Workshops, those who formed various writing groups over the years, some of whom have been both former students and/or teaching colleagues, and guest poets who inspired me.

Colleagues during my forty-year teacher career in Prince William County for supporting me and challenging me to grow.

Students in my Graham Park Middle and Woodbridge Senior High

School English, Language Arts, and Creative Writing classes, especially those I taught multiple years in the Center for the Fine and Performing Arts (CFPA) and those I advised on the *Eddas* Literary/Art Magazine and *Eddas* Coffee House staff. They brought me joy and enhanced my writing education.

Members of The Poetry Society of Virginia, The Prince William Poet Laureate Circle, The Virginia Women's Poetry Collective, Spilled Ink, Write-by-the Rails, and the DC area poetry community who have supported and encouraged me.

Readers of *I'd Rather Be a Hyacinth*: Angela Dribben for helping me re-envision manuscript order and inviting me to be a part of the Virginia Women's Poetry Collective; Roxanne French, for reading early drafts and revisions and being my "P.R. rep"; Kathy Smaltz for careful reading, perspective, and commitment to learning at many Dodge Poetry Festivals.

Grace Cavalieri and Kathy Smaltz for beautiful book blurbs.

A native of Northern Virginia, **Cathy Hailey** teaches as an adjunct lecturer in Johns Hopkins University's online MA in Teaching Writing program. Previously she taught English and Creative Writing in Prince William County (PWC), VA, for forty years, her favorite years as part of the Center for the Fine and Performing Arts Creative Writing Program. She sponsored the award-winning *Eddas* Literary/Art Magazine for thirty-three years.

Hailey graduated from Duke University with an AB (*Artium Baccalaureus*) in English and earned an MA in English, with a concentration in Professional Writing and Editing, from George Mason University. She has been a Teacher-Consultant for the Northern Virginia Writing Project (NVWP) since 1981 and later co-directed with a focus on the Student Summer Institute and Young Writers Workshops. In 2010, she won the Mark Farrington Personal Writing Award, which supported her first attendance at the Geraldine Dodge Poetry Festival, inspiring her to prioritize her own poetry writing.

As a member of the Prince William Poet Laureate Circle, Hailey organizes, In the Company of Laureates, a biennial reading of poets laureate held in PWC. She serves as Northern Region Vice President of The Poetry Society of Virginia. For PSV, she hosts Where Art Meets the Line, a poetry reading series featuring poet artists, and she cohosts Virginia Voices, a monthly poetry reading and interview series. She enjoys collaborations with poets, visual artists, and musicians, including Springtime in Winter, Peace & Identity, Tapestry of Peace & Justice, and DC Unsettled. She was invited as a guest poet to The Word Works' final Joaquin Miller Poetry program, an event honoring Jacklyn Potter.

Hailey's writing has been published in *The New Verse News, Poetry Virginia, Written in Arlington, Stay Salty: Life in the Garden State* (Vol. 2), *Poetry for Ukraine* (THE POET), *Family* (THE POET), and *NoVA Bards*. Poems are forthcoming in *The Poetry Society of Virginia Centennial Anthology*.